THE TRUE ACCOUNT

OF MYSELF

AS A BIRD

THE TRUE ACCOUNT

OF MYSELF

AS A BIRD

ROBERT WRIGLEY

PENGUIN POETS

PENGUIN BOOKS

An imprint of Penguin Random House LLC

penguinrandomhouse.com

LIBRARY OF CONGRESS CATALOGING-IN-PUBLICATION DATA

Names: Wrigley, Robert, 1951– author.

Title: The true account of myself as a bird / Robert Wrigley.

Description: New York : Penguin Books, [2022] | Series: Penguin poets

Identifiers: LCCN 2021044141 (print) | LCCN 2021044142 (ebook) | ISBN 9780143137245 (paperback) | ISBN 9780593511190 (ebook)

Subjects: LCGFT: Poetry.

Classification: LCC PS3573.R58 T78 2022 (print) | LCC PS3573.R58 (ebook) | DDC 811/.54—dc23

LC record available at https://lccn.loc.gov/2021044141

LC ebook record available at https://lccn.loc.gov/2021044142

Printed in the United States of America

1st Printing

Set in New Caledonia LT Std

Designed by Sabrina Bowers

for my mother,

BETTY ANN WRIGLEY,

who also gave me my love of words and birds

All we are not stares back at what we are.

—W. H. AUDEN

CONTENTS

THE TRUE ACCOUNT
OF MYSELF
AS A BIRD

WHY THE NIGHT BIRD SINGS

This bird, whatever bird it is,
sings on melodious and monotonous

and never tells a truth or a lie, not one.
At its end, just as when it began,

the night bird's song is something else,
no more true or false than wind or bells.

And if you were the bird, your poem
would be the song and where it comes from,

yourself and a tree
in the night, and the night would be

a dark page the ink
that is your poem sinks in

and disappears, almost like the sky
out of which the bird sings. That's why.

SYNOVIAL

"Joint fluid," declared the physician—spilled
          from a sprung seal in the ultimate knuckle
of my left index finger, and gathered there,
          just shy of the nail, to a "myxoid cyst"—
a substance also called "digital mucus."
          Once a woman with beautiful hands
assured me, "There are very few physical pleasures
          without a little mucus."
But when this doctor with an expensive
          lancet lanced it, there oozed from my myxoid cyst
a viscid substance vastly more limpid than semen
          or vaginal secretions. It was like a luminous tear
wept by a fly-sized golden butterfly,
          and when I touched the tiny glistening orb of it
with the pad of my opposite index finger, it clung
          to the print's whorls, and when I swirled it
against the pad of my thumb I knew
          my body will never repay me
for the satisfactions I give it every day by moving.
          O itty-bitty pure lubricious gobbet,
O most licentious and merest whit betwixt the pads
          of index finger and thumb
slid so lusciously together the joints between my carpal
          and metacarpal bones thrummed a hum
in the heart of every atom of my corpus,
          from just this side of corpsehood all the way back
to the slither and divot of my conception,
          which the doctor, seeing the look on my face,
closed his eyes before the lust and rapture of.

OLD PAN

for lost boys

Windblown seedpod parasols lofted
from a withered western salsify blossom drift past me
in a cloud of silken Tinker Bells, a shitload even. Forgive me,

that's just the sort of word my brain seizes upon
when I'm on the roof of the shack, sweeping off
half a haystack of pine needles and wondering what on earth

I'm doing here so far above the earth
at the age of seventy. The needles
have woven themselves to a kind of raffia mat that would,

if I were to step on it, sled off
down the slanted steel beneath me and cushion
my seven-yard fall hardly at all. So, sweep a little,

step a little, sweep a little, step. Then this
blizzard of Brobdingnagian dandelion fluffs,
and I think to myself, *Sweet heavens, Tinker Bells!*

before remembering that ill-timed words
could break me too—swiftly if I'm lucky.
But my oh my, how I fell at twelve for the sleek, bewinged

and leggy little Tinker Bell on the Disneyfied big screen.
Just think how Tink wished woman-sized and flying
could solve today's pine needle problem in a trice.

True, *trice* sounds like a wisp of swimwear but is in fact defined
as "to hoist," and also as "an instant of time"—about as long as
a hoisted fool would take to drop twenty feet.

This is when my wife, not wishing to check
on me through the window, checks on me
through the window and perceives me propped

Astaire-like on a push broom and leaned a little too far out
trying to catch from the storm of salsify seeds asail around me
just one. No, no, I'm not grinning, I'm concentrating.

Nobody in the world ever wanted to grow up
believing this much in words,
even a paltry man upon a push broom, somehow still in love.

PREY

May 2, 2019,

with a couple of clauses by Robert Mueller

Funny how, yesterday, seeing the attorney general lie
has led me, in a weird if sleepy rage,
to spend almost an hour this morning

watching an enormously pregnant whitetail doe
browse among the new spring leaves and grasses.
I'd meant to focus my ire where it would prove useless—

a letter to one of my wholly owned corporate senators,
the one who'll take me fishing with him
for a contribution of fifteen thousand dollars.

Twin fawns, for sure, maybe triplets. I would like
to fully capture the context, nature, and substance
of her, how at ease she seems despite the fact

that I'm no more than a stone's half throw away.
She watched me come out onto the deck
and stopped her chewing until I was in my chair.

Now the pages of my notebook flutter in the breeze.
I want to be clear. I do not want public confusion
about critical aspects: the way she is sleek

but also rotund, how she glistens with morning dew.
Even here, among scattered American houses
on a mountainside in Idaho, she is not safe,

nor will her fawns be safe when they are born.
She is a prey animal and predators abound,
still it is also true she has never been lied to.

MOSS LOVES BONE TO DEATH

But the mice who live in the gray whale's skull
must adore its plush and shingling, the purchase
their tiny feet are afforded, the carpeted blowhole
skylight, and the gap where the left eye was,
draped against the wind, the primary entryway.

Some days from the kitchen window, the ground
around it's a hullabaloo of nestlings' first forays
in the sun, and their eerie, busy chittering sounds.

Call it first mercy, the many minds of moss, bone
delivering unto the dreams of moss its green,
the cat offering upon the welcome mat, one
by one, dozens of carcasses at full skull production,
as though a whale ghost had imagined them there,
little whale thoughts, also dead, in waterless air.

BE GLAD

For days bumblebees and hummingbirds
hummed and bumbled
among the brightly colored camp goods
as though each item were
a pollen-sweet blossom, just as I

myself and my guitar
appeared to be
to the black swallowtail butterfly
yesterday afternoon, the way
it wandered us, my guitar and me.

Knuckles, wedding band, the wound
on the back of my left
index finger, just below the nail—
it investigated them all,
working around my playing.

The inlaid fret markers drew it too,
although the strings' vibrations
perturbed it again and again.
The perches provided by the tuning posts
attracted it awhile as well.

It unrolled its odd black
tongue or proboscis to test
the pitch or pith of every nub of string.
Meanwhile, we played a slow,
almost mournful version

of the Beatles' "She Loves You,"
not exactly a sad song,
even as the butterfly roamed
across us, my guitar and me.
Hottest day of the summer so far.

A pair of cedar waxwings
hunted bugs above the river,
and wisely or luckily
the swallowtail avoided that air,
choosing to study me and my guitar.

As for the "you" she loves—
yeah-yeah-yeah, not the hurting kind—
was he a Lennon or a McCartney
or just an every any man,
scourge of many popular songs?

When at last I moved on
from "She Loves You" to "You Don't Know Me,"
recorded by Ray Charles when I was eleven,
the swallowtail,
exclusively a Beatles fan, it seemed,

flew away and disappeared.
Today I'm not playing guitar at all,
and my red mechanical pencil
has attracted a hummingbird
and a bumblebee

but not one butterfly
of any sort, neither a black swallowtail
nor a yellow, not even

one of those small blue-and-white ones
I do not know the name of,

the kind that lands on your bare feet
still wet from wading boots,
of whose touch you are hardly even aware,
though six or more wander your toes,
administering kisses as light as air.

NARRATING NIGHT TO
THE NEW PUPPY GLADYS

Here we have shadows and over there rain
to drive down the dust till dust comes again.

Now there's wind that once was a breeze.
Just wait and see what it does to the trees.

More dark shows up as the power goes down
and all the lights vanish from here to town

and the fridge where your food is quits its hum,
the music strangles, the radio's dumb.

You stretch and yawn, give your ears a flap,
then fart and circle back down on my lap.

A pink-bellied four months old are you,
I'm hairy and eight hundred fifty-two.

But don't worry, this is only the end of the poem,
all the stuff about humans, family, and home.

No, your paws, they're balm; your nose, pure salve;
and your life span might be more years than I have.

Sleep on, sweet Gladys, have a dream or two.
Someday you'll mourn me or I'll mourn you.

WHAT IT'S GOOD FOR

"This is the choil. It's the part of the blade
at the very bottom of the sharpened edge,
where the sharpening ceases.

Kind of a curb, there to keep
the handle from being scratched
by the stone during sharpening,"

said my friend, the knife-lover.
"No," said the knife-maker
behind the table, "that's called the ricasso."

And while my friend blushed,
I asked the other man, "Is that an Italian
word?" And he answered, most authoritatively,

"Yes, it is. It means the place
at the base of the blade that is not sharpened."
But I liked *choil* better, and it seemed

later that night, my friend consulting knife books
and I the *OED*, that the two words
were more or less synonyms, often presented

together, with a slash between them,
sometimes as *ricasso/choil*, others as *choil/
ricasso*. It hardly mattered, really.

It was the part of the knife no one cared about,
except those who love knives or make knives,
of which I was not one. I like a good knife

but I loved the word *choil*. And even *ricasso,*
the more I said it, sounded delicious.
So I was grateful to my friend,

the lover of knives, and to the knife-maker too,
for giving me these words I would slip away
as though into a sheath or scabbard, awaiting

the moment one or the other, or even both
of them, might occur to me, in exactly the right
situation, perhaps in response to someone

on an airplane, frustrated by the final clues
of a crossword puzzle and in desperation asking
the distinguished-looking man next to him—

the one reading the biography of Jim Bowie—
who could be you since now you know the words,
though in this case it is I. And I'd slide my glasses

slowly down my nose, look not at the puzzle
but directly into the player's eyes,
and ask, "Seven letters or five?"

Although, it has been years now—more than twenty—
and no one has ever so inquired.
Then, today, looking through my desk drawer

for a toothpick, I find this old pocketknife,
manufactured by the Imperial Company, in Ireland,
and I pull out the blade, which my late father-in-law,

whose knife it was, must have sharpened a thousand times,
it is worn so thin. And there's the thing itself,
near the haft, which is another word for handle.

RODEO

This time of year, last weeks of winter every year,
the ant known among laypersons
as the "little black ant" and among myrmecologists
as *Monomorium minimum* marches through
the many hair-breadth fissures on the west side
of my shack and wanders the wall and the window
there in such numbers as would be alarming
to those who know not the little black ants' behaviors,
the weird aimlessness of their meanders
and their startling propensity, in the midst of so massive
an invasion, to vanish back into the cracks
and portals that emitted them moments before,
leaving behind only the one that has climbed
onto my notebook to engage the tip
of my pencil in battle,
then hoisting itself astride my writing hand,
waving its tiny ant Stetson and calling out
in the sonic range of its kind, *Yeehaw-yahoo-yeehaw!*

HORSE HEAVEN

The pipe from the spring cistern, beloved by birds
  for its chill on hot summer days, spilled
into a two-hundred-gallon trough made of coopered
  two-inch-thick wooden staves. And the trough was beloved
by a pair of frogs and two lazy geldings. Or not lazy
  but spoiled, infrequently ridden, fed every morning
a quarter bucket each of oat mix and molasses
  and every afternoon or evening an apple, carrot, or frozen slab
of watermelon rind. And the horses themselves were beloved
  by cowbirds, perched on the withers or the croup,
from which they'd pluck up the occasional otherwise
  horse-annoying insect. And the cowbirds rode across
the pasture to the trough that day, where I stood
  as I often stood with apples or sugar cubes in my pocket.
They perched on the horses to the north of the trough,
  while I stood on the south, one bird each remaining
but having at the sight of me retreated
  almost to the dock, the uppermost trace of the tail.
And we waited. Two horses, two birds, two frogs
  having dived to the bottom, and a man with a pocketful of sugar cubes.
They were beginning to understand the drill, the horses.
  I wanted them to drink first. They knew it, but they were impatient.
First one then the other dipped his snout in the water
  and looked up at me, hopeful, ready, though I waited,
my arms folded over my chest. I wanted to see them drink,
  and soon they did, lapping, then plunging their muzzles deep
below the surface to gulp, sometimes in the process remembering
  how thirsty they must have been and taking in great drafts,
pints or more, although eventually one stopped
  and lifted his head, then the other, and I produced

two sugar cubes from my pocket and arranging one on each palm
           held them out, and their soft horse lips
and cold tongues lifted the cubes into their mouths
           and I heard a single crunch and watched as joy
swept across their faces. When I produced two more
           we repeated the process. Then we waited again.
Because I did not walk away they believed I still had more,
           as I did, but still I waited. And the frogs swam in the trough,
and the cowbirds hunted bugs near the docks,
           then one by one the horses both drank again, less than before,
then lifted their heads and looked at me.
           Spoiled, yes, and probably lazy too. Two geldings we owned
for several years, having rescued them from a stable
           where they sometimes spent days at a time in their stalls,
mouthing a meal of tasteless hay from a rick, a draft of murky water
           from a bucket on a hook—nothing like the spill
of this cold and continually fresh spring. They had not died
           but they understood they had gone to horse heaven.
There was a seven-acre pasture of tall grass. Often at night
           there was a moon. There were apples and carrots
and frozen watermelon rinds, and there was the man I was,
           waiting with them, waiting for them now, as they waited
for and with me, and at last when one of them nickered
           or shook a head—those immemorial equine interrogatories—
and I produced from my miraculous pocket two final cubes of sugar
           they ate with a look of trembling ecstasy,
after which I walked back to the house
           and sat on the porch and waited for them,
as they always did on such days and as they did that day,
           to run around the pasture once or twice in their joy,
which was beloved by me.

TEMPEST

When your mama so soon returned to work
her heavenly breast milk reheated
had to be nursed through a silicone nipple

the color of earwax
and by the look on your little outraged face the flavor too.
Though it became a battle barely to breathe,

you wailed and wailed. Even when I walked you
on my shoulder or bounced you at my knees,
you'd only sometimes stop awhile and snub,

then set off weeping yet again. After a time we'd try
the bottle once more, both of us
less hopeful than before, until at last,

to the mercy of cruel fate resigned, you latched upon
the wretched thing, though deep and vast was your despair.
And your gift. For once, wholly shot through,

I bowed my head, and there fell from my cheek
to yours a tear that startled you
from the stupor of a half-hearted suckle—

and your lower lip quivered, as though you'd cry again.
Then you saw me, or recognized me, or in my father face knew
what you were and for all my life would be to me.

BONE PILE

Having fetched home bones for years,
and having fashioned from them
handles, bird perches, whirligigs, and what all;

having in the process accumulated lesser ones
and seconds, some unshapely, some blunt
or mouse-gnawed in haphazard inartful ways,

I have made from my bone gleanings this
as well: an anthill catacomb, an ossified fortress
of parapets and keeps a mouse king nightly strides.

Bone of deer, bone of moose. Bone of bear,
bobcat, coyote, and lynx. Unidentifiable bone
found mid-meadow, not a single other around.

Bird bones, bone slivers, bone spurs and sprouts.
Spoonlike wings of ilia, sprocketed vertebrae,
an upthrust arc of mid-rib ravens like to clamp onto

like the high priests of bones they've always been.
Skulls bashed and bullet-shattered, mandibles
and maxillae shedding teeth like dice.

I would have my own bones added to it someday,
if it were allowed. A year or two on a funeral platform,
until the birds and blowflies have done

their thorough work, then the bigguns pitched singly,
little ones poured by xylophonic sackfuls, skull
planted pate down, to cackle at the sun, moon, and stars.

AFTER A LONG DRY SPELL

You're able to count the drops
at first, soft explosions in dust,
slaps on grasses dry as withered crops,
bonging metal things, threatening rust.

Also on your cheeks, your uncombed hair,
until they are too many to count:
not a drop in three months or more—
then drip, then patter, now a drenching pour.

You're naked, it's true, but so what?
You heard a drop smack the window,
and barely awake you ran out
to stand like an unclothed scarecrow,

straw-colored, arms open wide
to receive it, rain at last, just for you.
And over there, on the east side,
your neighbor, waving, naked too.

ON A LATE FLIGHT EAST FROM SEATTLE

Looking down on the darkness
of the Cascades for a few seconds
I saw the moon shining in a mountain lake

and wondered if anyone else had seen it too—
some other insomniac passenger
or perhaps the copilot.

Probably no one but me.
Three or four seconds looking down
on the shimmering silver moon, full and round,

shining up from the surface of a cold mountain lake
then gone, the actual moon
in the midst of stars invisible above the plane,

on a smooth flight, as from a row behind
the barely perceived but unmistakable sound
of a kiss, and then a sigh.

HUMMINGBIRD ON THE WIRE

the boredom of God / is heartbreaking
—LEONARD COHEN

Humming "Bird on the Wire,"
I notice there's an actual
hummingbird on the wire

that keeps the feeder
high above the bear, the feeder that dangles
below the hummingbird on the wire.

June, and it's hungry, this bear,
and made uneasy as I thump the windowsill,
humming "Bird on the Wire."

O preternatural and eerie mild winter
that left for bears little winterkill,
even as the hummingbird on the wire

drives off all the other hummers
and will not share the feeder's sweet red spill.
I'm humming "Bird on the Wire"

when it stands up and waves a paw, the hungry bear.
No bear food near here, no bear food anywhere.
Just a hummingbird on the wire,
and me, humming "Bird on the Wire."

AK-47 CANDELABRUM

for Mark Solomon and the Peace Art Project,
Cambodia, 2004

Even if the paints and canvases, clay
and kilns, brushes and knives still
were there, all the old artists are bones
gone to soil in the killing fields.
Therefore let automatic rifles be also unbodied,
and let a simple bellows blow some coals
to their productive blood colors,
and let there likewise be the snouts,
horns, and blocks of anvils
over which might be shaped this abundance
of dead deathmaking machines,
that the living children may learn to make from them
shells and faces, trees and blossoms,
animals of myth and magic, and even this
tender steel hand holding over a table
on a mountaintop in Idaho
these four mild lights.

BOY KNEW I

Having with great stealth acquired the first
Playboy magazine ever would he possess,
from the back seat of a rattletrap four-door DeSoto
belonging to an older boy who played
with older other boys a game of basketball,

he aftertheftward and at great speed walked
through all the shortcuts furtive
with it under his secreted T-shirt
of the neighborhood, where
the problem it might by him be hidden

from his mother occurred to him, since from her never
anything successfully had he hidden yet before.
Thus atop the sheet metal cold air furnace return
down hung from the joists below
the floorboards slipped it he from his hand

while standing on the step top seat
of a step stool almost no one ever stepped
upon nor sat but him, who thereafter incessantly
seemed for retrieval to need it
and the it that was retrieved with it thereby.

Ah, convenience in that house of the basement
bathroom and the showers prolonged therein
for some many months,
until for a reason to him unknown
he forgot about the magazine and remembered it

only a week after from that house
they moved to another away,

and bereft at the thought he was by his loss.
For a time seeming long then in passing,
he bathed with assistance subsidiary

only of the memory had of it
by him, the *Playboy* he had stolen
and successfully in spite of his mother
all-knowing otherwise had hidden.
As for the so-called hard-core porno mag purloined

by him from a friend whose father such
magazines in great number mostly unhidden
in so-called his office had, different exceedingly
were its pictures, his curiosity dire and pained, so much
so the pictures' purpose for him almost could not suffice.

This magazine he in a plastic bag had hidden
in the rattletrap abandoned tree house of the long-gone boy
at the new place, where by spring rain incessant
and nest-building squirrels,
chewed and saturated swiftly it became,

until there only one picture was
that for his purposes somewhat useful remained.
But about it he forgot, of course,
in the back of his jeans pocket,
his laundry-doing mother

in the ordinary ransackery of all his hands
might have in such pocket places placed,
found it she and presented to him it,
then at him looked and looked
saying about it nothing more.

DAWN, UPPER WALTON LAKE

Selway-Bitterroot Wilderness, 2011

What was the wolf thinking, seeing me
from the lake's opposite shore
just as I saw it, though surely it saw me before?
Standing mostly undressed me, peeing me,

smelling exactly like what I was, am,
and always will be me. I was thinking,
It's cold, it's almost sunrise—then a slinking
on the other side: wait, not it, but two: them.

So what were the wolves thinking? And why,
when I made the least move—shaking the dew
off the lily, so to speak, as I always do—
did both begin to trot under a gray sky

across the bouldered moraine, headed east
into the deeper wild? Trot became
lope and they vanished among stones the same
shade as themselves, after which I noticed

all through camp, up to and around our tents,
their tracks, everywhere. They must have come
before first light, where they took in some
clearer awareness of us, and then went,

circumnavigating a high mountain lake,
when in mild light they saw me—I must have looked
exactly like it smelled I would—and they took
off at a trot, then a lope, time being theirs to take.

BLACK AND WHITE

The memory is not entirely false
but only almost visually true,
since the tires on the Mercury were clearly whitewalls,
although the car was not gray but green. Or possibly blue.

What I remember best is my father,
who took the picture—car, mother, sister, me.
He wore a new suit a shade of mortar,
color of the sidewalk that had scraped my scabbed knee.

Father's suit and sidewalk the same pale gray,
along a palette that holds everything we see—
'57 Mercury, scabbed knee, noon on a sunny day,
Easter, in the foreground one not-quite-white peony.

MIGHT HAVE BEEN JULY,
MIGHT HAVE BEEN DECEMBER

More oblique the eagle's angle
than the osprey's precipitous fall,
though rose up both and under them dangled
a trout, the point of it all.

Festooned, a limb on each one's
favorite tree either side of the river,
with chains of bone and lace of skin
the river's wind made shiver.

Sat under them both, one in December,
one in July, in distinct seasonal air,
and once arrived home, as I remember,
with a thin white fish rib lodged in my hair.

AN EVERYWHERE AT ONCE

Scarved in morning mist, the river's smithed
its own gold necklace of larch needles.
Sometimes she's a woman, the river,
lean and strong and luscious and cold,
ripe sometimes, mostly naked, never old.
Look awhile at her froths and laces,
depths and curves and swells in her bed.

And know it is a rare stillness if it reflects you,
and an illusion in any case,
since where you are is only a place,
while the river is an everywhere at once,
headwaters to toes—all along
the lap and plunge
she shimmers like every eye that ever was.

TRACKS OF A HARE IN NEW SNOW

Down the driveway, along the path to the shack,
then up seven stairs to the porch,
until they disappear under a bench
where the hare must have sheltered
for the night, or for a while at least, leaving
only a few pellets on the boards beneath
and, curiously, no tracks showing it ever departed,

causing me to conclude it is still there
and chameleoned from its winter white
to its under-the-bench-on-bare-boards invisibility—
twitching its long whiskers, one ear
cocked toward the window I watch from
and the other aimed outward in the vain hope
of hearing in its descent the snowy invisible owl.

I WANT TO PRAISE HER PARTS

I want to praise her parts—helm,
gorget, plackart, greave—but her wounds
(sudden gust, window) suggest more
than exoskeletal dishevelment and worry me.
Even my lying on my belly on the porch,
looming over and looking at her
through a magnifying glass, does not make her
leap or fly. If she can. She's almost an inch long,
her antennae upright and gently curved, her thighs
(if that's what they are, the muscular-seeming
upper parts of her cricket legs) tense
and tapered. Large hypnotic black eyes,
the long stiletto of her ovipositor.
A dozen shades of amber, she is. I would like
to kiss her, she is so clear to me through the glass.
Then I see her left ear, just below the knee
of her foreleg, elongate, lighter hued,
and I cannot take my eyes from it.
When she rotates a quarter inch away
from me and appears to be gathering herself
to leap and fly, it turns out she doesn't,
which may or may not be
because I have begun softly to sing.

TO THE MAN

I was a songbird, one of the kind
whose name I do not know, plain
of plumage but with a mellifluous

many-noted song. I was on the deer
bone perch outside the window,
and it seemed I was singing to myself

inside, that I was watching myself
singing, and that I was hearing
myself singing to the man I was,

as though I were the bird and not the man
I would be when I woke and forgot,
as I always do, and which I did.

Although now I am convinced this is
the true account of myself as a bird
alighted on the perch that is the rib

of a deer, seeming to sing for the man
I would have to be, yet again,
when this too must end.

THE CONSCIOUSNESS OF EVERYTHING

from children's questions

Consider the happiness of an empty hand
from which the horse has taken a carrot,
or the house that sits on once-empty land
and the land that now loves to bear it.

What does sun feel for a shadow?
The horse's hoof for the shoe of steel?
Which loves most for the car to go,
the people inside or the wheels?

The mirror, smitten with the left-handed man,
offers a right-handed one in return.
Spoon loves soup and soup the can,
and the log in the stove lives to burn.

Of its stink the stink bug's especially fond
while stink's a fan of the stink bug too.
Frog spawn delights in the murk of the pond,
and one is infatuated with zero and two.

Two's enchanted by four and six
and all six sides love the cube.
Snow digs cold and ice likes its slicks
but toothpaste despises the tube.

My daughter asked, "Is the wind a girl?"
and I told her she sure must be,
since wind is brave and travels the world,
delighting her brother the weather. And trees.

Time's almost gone now when a stone could hurt,
when a feather missed its wing,
when sky kissed clouds and grass held dirt
and nothing thought itself just a thing.

I take my time in the woods today
saying hello to every this and that,
as though the world might still be that way,
when my head beguiled my hat.

MACHINERY

My father loved every kind of machinery,
relished bearings, splines, windings, and cogs,
loved the tolerances between moving parts
and the parts that moved the parts,
the many separate machines of machinery.
Loved the punch, the awl, the ratchet, the pawl.
Infeed and outfeed rollers of the thickness planer,
its cutter head and cutters. The barrel and belt sanders,
the auger, capstan, windlass, and magneto.
Such a beautiful vocabulary in his work, words
he knew even if often he did not know
how they were spelled. Seals, risers, armatures.
Claw, ball-peen, sledge, dead-blow, mallet,
hammers all. Butt, mitered, half-lap,
tongue and groove; mortise and tenon,
biscuit, rabbet, dovetail, and box: all joints.
"A poem is a small (or large) machine
made of words," said William Carlos Williams.
"Building the machine that makes the machine,"
said Elon Musk. Once my father repaired
a broken harpsichord but could not make it sing.
The chock, the bore, the chisel. He could hang a door,
rebuild an engine. Cylinders, pistons, and rings.
Shafts, crank and cam. Hand-cut notches
where the hinges sat. He loved the primary feathers
on the wings of a duck, extended and catching air,
catching also the tops of the whitecap waves
when it landed. Rods, valves, more risers, more seals.
Ailerons and flaps, yaw control in the tail.
Machinery, machinery, machinery, machinery.
Four syllables in two iambic feet. A soft pulse.

Once I told him what Williams said,
he approached what I made with deeper interest
but no more understanding in the end.
The question he did not ask, that would have
embarrassed him to ask, the question I knew
he wanted to ask, the one I was too embarrassed
to ask for him, was "What does it do?"
Eventually the machine, his body, was broken,
and now it is gone, and the mechanically inclined
machine in his head is also gone,
and most of his tools, the machines that made
the machines, are gone too, but for a few
I have kept in remembrance. A fine wood plane
but not the thickness planer, which I would not know
how to use. A variety of clamps I use to clamp
things-needing-clamping clamped. Frost said
poetry is "the sort of thing poets write." My father
thought it was the sort of thing I wrote,
but what mattered to him was what it did.
And what does it do? A widget that resists
conclusions. A crank that turns a wheel
that turns. A declaration of truth
by a human being running at full speed
in a race with no one, toward nowhere
except away from the beginning toward arrival.
Once my father watched the snow
and noted how landing on the earth it melted.
He said, "It's snow that doesn't know it's rain."

BARN

Moonspokes through the old roof shakes showed
her chest freckled with silver. She observed a drop
of light creeping and retreating down and up
his right shoulder. The stallion stamped
then kicked the door, a concentrated thundercrack,
and the mare to be covered tomorrow nickered
consolations or come-hithers, their heads extended
to the withers through the windows of their stalls.

Dust rose in the spokes, and she rolled over
and slung herself across a saddle. A dime of light
tried to etch the face of FDR between her shoulder blades.
In the horses' enormous eyes they were shadows
the dust they made beglistened. The horses were quiet then,
listening, and the wheel of the moon
rolled silent as light over what they saw.

THE FLOWER OF ALL WATER

—Roethke

1.

You went back to the land of your birth,
and lo, you were miserable, and pined
and whined and sulked with aggressive silences,
until the people who loved you most were gladdest
to see you go, and you went back to where
you could have been happy if you'd already been,
and lo, you were not happy but miserable
except in a different way than before,

until you were not and became, between periods
of misery as common as weather, glad
to be both where you were and who,
and happiness came and went and came
again and went again like weather
in all the miserable lands of men.

2.

During your exile you studied topographical maps
like skin. An imagined landscape
became your lover. You rhapsodized
so extravagantly two of your friends moved
to the mountains the next year. Would they forgive you,
would they love you, would they wonder
how unhappy they must have been
to move sixteen hundred miles away at the urgings

of someone as lamentable and doleful as yourself?
Still, there were mountain lakes no trail came near,

and some of those you would visit on your own.
Miles from anyone. You were never afraid.
You saw things miraculous and wild.
You'd never been so perfectly lonely in your life.

    3.

Here, at the end of a double-broken line
the map's legend defines
as an "unimproved road," the unimproved road ends.
Here you find a mile of single-broken line,
a trail that trudges across the field of another map,
and here is the trailless ridge you clamber up to
and traverse, crawling over and hiking around
boulders and twenty-foot ravines

too shallow to show in contour lines,
then the field of rocks as big as houses down
the slope to the lake so remote no one yet
has given it a name, nor the mountain
south of it, over which you watched the moon rise,
and in the lee of which the moonlight ravished you.

    4.

At the headwall, where the snowfield stood
for all time, hidden from the sun,
where eagles scattered bones—
voles and pikas in the eyes of the clouds
and trout given away by the moon—
here you learned the moment wax
turns wane, calculated every full moon
of your life against the number seen,

and saw the flower of all water
and the water of every flesh,
and saw your shadow shade a thousand blazes
of quartz on the shoreline ledge,
where the moon illuminated a translucent trout
and a cluster of bones deep underwater.

5.

It seems the land of your death
is just as likely there, at the end of the long shaft
of moonlight, a simulacrum of your life.
Only at the petals on the surface
can you breathe, neither in the plummet
nor having drowned. Only in the membrane
of gladness, the intoxications of weather,
the never-long-enough caress of the sun or the moon.

Sing awhile. Accentuate the silence,
study constellations you invent when left to your own.
Every map believes it is a metaphor.
One night you dream you find your own bones
in a meadow beside a river
and lie down beside them until happiness lies with you.

DONE

Dawn, second most lovely
awakening of the day, he thinks.
As he thinks the light—so lately
illuminating slopes with golds and pinks—
by ripening to its singular glow,
diminishes itself but makes its effect,
also singular, all the more so.

For now what's lit by sun reflects
on what he reflects upon every day
at dawn, his wonder undiminished,
made more clear as any last gray
is driven out, and night is finished,
and he watches. But just to see.
Only that, and no more, considerately.

BIG SHOES

It's the day after Thanksgiving,
and chaos reigns among the thrift store shoes,
wing tips sprawled side by side
with the baby booties. What I came for

is mukluks to leave in the pickup,
but what I'm struck by is a pair
of bright red, impossibly high, sling-back stilettos,
the sexiest shoes I have ever seen, except

they're enormous. Size 16.
Worn some too. The tiny pads on the heels
ooze a little to the outsides, some
substantial scuffing at the balls,

as though for one long night
they'd been relentlessly danced in.
Who wouldn't imagine the woman
who'd danced in such shoes? Or the man.

Probably I didn't need to pull
my pant legs up when I tried them on,
and I probably did not need to try them both,
but I did. My feet are not wide but still

the shoes were exceedingly tight across the toes,
while the backs of my heels—slid
down the shoes' steep slopes—
sat over an inch from the thin back strap.

They were hard to stand in, of course,
and I took only a few steps back
and forth before looking up to see
one of my fellow shoppers watching me.

A former student, it turned out. Adam,
who favors black greatcoats and fingerless gloves,
whose ears are massively gauged
and abundantly studded, tattoos of three

blue tears descending his left cheek.
He smiled and remarked that they seemed
a little big for me. I smiled back
and fumbled them off, then he said,

"There's a poem in this, isn't there?"
There is, Adam, there is, and this is it.
I'm glad your Thanksgiving was a happy one,
and even gladder you did not think

to reach for your phone until
the shoes were off and back on the rack.
But I was after a hint, a vision,
and my feet where those feet had been

have given me *this*—not the whole
surely spectacular length of her, but a glimpse,
the merest glimpse, of the men she, or maybe he,
would have danced with, one of whom looked

just a little like you,
then quite late that night
one of the others,
who looked a lot like me.

PRAISE BOB

623 S. 3rd St. West, Apt. 3, Missoula, 1974

The fact that our first names, the young man I was
and the young man who lived in the apartment below mine,
should be the same meant little to me,

until the night someone in his bed
woke me with the most musical moans, then cried out,
O Bob, O Bob, O Bob! No sleep for me after that.

The next morning I rose before sunrise,
made coffee, and sat at the kitchen window,
hoping to get a glimpse of the one who had called.

But no one ever showed except Bob himself,
dark-haired, of medium build, wearing a red tie
and a black jacket, carrying a lunch box shaped like a barn.

He strolled a foot above the ground
and brought forth with a quick flick of his wrist
an already lit and half-smoked cigarette.

Then he stopped and turned back to his apartment door,
toward which he gave the merest nod, and a wink,
then spun to a blur and ascended into the clouds.

BISON

The shyest wind walks among them
as they graze, can even be seen
urging them along, herding them almost,

among the vastnesses. Placid, massive,
theirs is the locomotion of planets
or stars, slow boulders in the river's quick.

All day they have come and gone, a million or more
similarly humped and haunched, their bellies
darkening blue, swollen with rain.

COME HOME

I had to lean the ladder against the eaves
and stand upon the third step up
to drive its ladderfeet down through snow.
Had to take the push broom up
to clear a way along the roof pitch to the flue,
which had to be swept likewise clear.
A chore that ought to have been done before
now had to be done at night. In a blizzard.
Had to wear a headlamp, had to thread
the four thirty-six-inch extension rods to the brush
and haul the twelve-plus feet
of bouncing apparatus up the ladder
to the flue. Had to pull the chimney cap
and see the throat of the stove choked
on creosote and fly ash. Had to drive
the seven-inch brush down the six-inch hole
twice and pull it back up, freckling
the roofsnow with black in the night.
Had to go inside and undo the flue pipe
and vacuum out the black and shining dust
with the Shop-Vac, then reconnect the flue.
Had to crumple newspaper and grid kindling
and light the fire. Had to dump the Shop-Vac's
black ghost behind the shed,
had to watch as snowfall
freckled the ash. Had to stand awhile
plastered with snow and ash, smelling woodsmoke.
Had to take the ladder down and put it away,
had to unthread the plunge rod into four pieces again
and rap the wire brush against a tree.
Had to leave boots in the garage

and blackened coat and pants in the laundry.
Went ahead and undressed entirely
and walked upstairs
with fly-ash-smeared face and sootified hands,
and had to wave at her as she sautéed some garlic.
Had to smile at her smile, had to shower.
Had to admit it was good to be home.

FIGURE

You want a piece of me
to see, from the depths of me,
a flesh from within me
no one's ever seen, not me,
nor the mother or the lovers of me.
A piece that will have been me,
then is no longer me,
but a synecdoche of me,

or possibly metonymy,
a figure of speech of me,
in contiguity or association with me,
a part for the whole of me,
a sliver that once was me,
so you might perceive the end of me.

VISITANT

The little building built on a slope
sits on piers, so I use the space
beneath it for storage, and I can tell
by the sound of the steps

of whatever it is that's down there
this late afternoon—walking around,
taking shelter from the snow—
not only exactly where it is

but what it's stepping on as it goes.
The shelf of spare lumber,
a rack that holds the chainsaws;
firewood, buckets of snow-melter,

roofing tar, polymeric mortar.
A retired charcoal grill. Whatever it is, it is,
it seems, unaware of me up here,
and I don't mind it down there.

The snow's approaching thirty inches deep,
it's eleven degrees. The problem is,
I have to pee, which will require not only
rolling my chair away from the desk

but walking across the way to the door,
then out onto the covered porch
and across the porch to the urinal.
The urinal's made of a transmission fluid funnel

that drains into a length of decommissioned
garden hose down into a shallow rock well.
I hate the unsightliness of yellow snow.
But I also hate to disturb whatever it is.

Whatever it is, it's moderately small, or not large—
raccoon, porcupine, maybe a marten, a badger,
even possibly (and this would be miraculous)
a wolverine, an animal I have seen only once

in my life. Another problem is, in my life
at this point, when I have to pee
it is not in my interests to put it off,
and I've been putting it off for quite a while now,

distracted as I listen (there it is among the buckets;
there on the lumber; there among the chainsaws),
but I'm hardly distractable anymore
and approaching, oh, mildly desperate,

squirming in my chair, finding it harder
to imagine where whatever it is is,
until I mutter "Sorry, pal" and go ahead
and stand, and walk to the door

and go outside and hurry across the porch
and stand before the urinal and unzip
and let loose and in the process heave
a loud sigh of relief, all the while still

listening, wondering which way whatever it is
will go, though now I wonder if
it will go, or if, as I had done inside, it will
hunker down, get very still,

and wait. After I'm done
and zipped up, I wait as well, standing
and listening and hearing nothing but the tick
of snow on the porch boards, a mild breeze

through the trees, a snowplow way out on the highway.
Has whatever it is already run? Has it left a path
through the snow? I go to the stairs
and descend three of seven steps

and crouch down to look. Nothing
on the shelf of spare lumber or among the buckets,
nothing nestled among the chainsaws.
But then I see it, or see its eyes, at least.

Whatever it is, it is crouched atop the firewood,
tucked between the floor joists
exactly at the place above which
the woodstove burns and must warm

if only by a few degrees the subfloor there.
It is black, I think, in the dim light, and fitted so snugly
into the space between the joists it has no shape,
it appears to be a ten-by-sixteen-inch rectangular animal

of very dark, possibly black, fur, a shiny black nose
and gleaming black eyes, eyeing me.
It's the cold that makes me shiver.
I'm coatless, after all, in a T-shirt and jeans,

wearing a pair of old house slippers.
"What are you?" I ask, and whatever it is
does not blink. Then I say, "Forgive me,
I'm sorry to bother you, please stay.

I just wish I knew what you are."
And though I do not know what it is,
I rise and go back inside
and toss another piece of firewood in the stove.

When I leave as evening's coming on,
whatever it is will be gone,
and though I will have listened,
I will not have heard it go.

LOVELY

Edinburgh, November 2013

Three train conductors pronounced our tickets so,
two waiters approved of our orders in their pubs,
and a clerk—when my wife, befuddled by the coinage,
held out a palm full of pounds and pence—

counted aloud, "One, three, four quid ten,"
and declared that amount, or the sweetness of her,
or the blueness of her eyes, just the same.
And the stranger who took the park bench beside us

one night in Newcastle, who smoked three cigarettes
as we sipped our champagne and whisky,
who told us half her life story and was told by us
half of ours, said "lovely" eleven times,

or maybe twelve. I might have missed one,
and now I miss them all. You don't hear it much
back home, except, lately, around our house,
the view from which has often been described

as beautiful, majestic, awesome, or amazing,
but hardly ever, as it seems this afternoon, lovely,
the sun going down and tomorrow even now arriving
right on time, midnight, 2400 GMT, over there,

roughly the time that night in Scotland,
when we sat on a hotel towel, under our umbrellas
on Lady Stair's Close, and a man nodded to us,
as he climbed toward High Street, and said it

mysteriously—an evaluation of the night
or of our chosen perch, or simply of us—
or rather, as it seemed it was, merely as a greeting,
so much better, so vastly superior to *hello.*

HOW ENORMOUS

I never saw the spider that bit me
on the heel of my left palm,
its sting no worse than a bee's.

But soon a tiny fluid-filled ulceration rose
that in a minute more was surrounded
by an inflamed, roseate corona.

Interesting to think about it,
being alone and feeling electric rushes
tunnel up into the cup of my palm,

then shimmer and diminish in my fingers.
A wipe of isopropyl with a cotton swab,
a smear of antibiotic ointment,

and a pour of good rye whiskey.
Stars coming on, a six-mile hike
back to the truck. What else was there to do?

We forget how enormous we are
even when the sky reminds us we're tiny.
I wondered, after the spider bit,

if it still clung to the stick of firewood
I tossed into the fire, and if it perished there.
Later, standing at the edge of camp,

I felt the world tilt. Something came close
and a chill rose up in me
that had to do with the spider too—

it was immense, heedless, everywhere,
no awareness whatsoever of me.
Probably nothing more than the dark.

PROTHALAMION

Putty knife from the toolbox,
water from the creek,
and a filthy sweat-stained T-shirt were all
that was needed to scrape and wipe
the mess from the windshield,
smack in the middle of the driver's
line of sight: an unrolled condom
and therefore likely a used one, melted
by afternoon sun but even molten
a recognizable thing. The car had been
at the trailhead for four days. There
was a firepit, a picnic table, and thousands of acres
of condom disposal space.
I had a three-hour drive home
after an eight-mile hike under a heavy pack
and four nights of sleeping on the ground,
but first the scraping and wiping,
then at last a barely cool beer
from the little ice chest.
When I took a seat at the picnic table,
I noticed the freshly carved heart,
"Dale + Amelia" inside. Also six
cigarette butts in the dirt underneath,
Camels all, three with red lipstick marks.
I have always liked the name Amelia
and up until that moment had been
ambivalent about Dale,
whose guilt beyond this circumstantial evidence
I could not be certain of. Nevertheless,
I also could not help imagining both
of them there, and Dale, in sun-dappled

afterglow, slipping off his sheath
and depositing it to the horror of Amelia
on my windshield.
Except, really, I hoped she didn't see
what he did with it at all, not even watching,
just looking at mountains and trees, listening to birds,
assuming he'd flung it into the brush
just as any other brutish lout would do,
while she sat at the picnic table,
lighting the first of three cigarettes,
and imagining, with Dale, of all men,
a long and romantic and happy life.

WHAT IT MEANS

Flicked from the camp table, the wing
of some kind of mayfly
spun dozens of times in its fall
and took five seconds to land on the ground.

What violence had sundered
the noble mayfly, so that
I should find and innocently flick
its wing from a folding table

from Costco and be amazed?
The immensity of Costco
and its always-open, or rather
somehow nonexistent, doors

causes birds to enter and never
return to the actual nonexistent sky.
Here, some bird did this mayfly flay
and slay and make a lunch

of mayfly head, legs, and thorax—
all but the now also lost wing,
which must have drifted
through the nonexistent sky

for many long minutes
to alight upon this table
from Costco, from the surface
of which I flicked its weightlessness,

and the wing swirled, fluttered, spun round
and round down to the ground to become
the ever-developing dazzling dust of earth,
among stars that are hardly there at all.

PERSEUS WITH THE HEAD OF MEDUSA

Except for the unfortunate head and hair, Cellini's
Medusa was a knockout. I remember that thought
occurring to me there, in the Piazza della Signoria,
but mentioning it to no one, meaning
I said not a word of it to Kim. I could have said,
Aveva un bel corpo, but she would have asked
what that meant. It also occurred to me
that Perseus, son of Zeus and heroic slayer
of the dreaded Gorgon, could not be said to be well-hung. At all.
I would guess I'm not the only man to whom
such thoughts have occurred in that place, and perhaps, like me,
most of the others kept their observations to themselves,
assuming they were men and not callow boys.
Or do the juvenile observations of callow boys
merely go, with time and caution, underground,
taking root in the brain and remaining unexpressed,
except silently, to himself, the mature aesthetic man?
The question must be, why am I saying it now?
Honesty's an answer, but not an especially good one.
Possibly admission, as in, yes, this is me,
this is the part of me I would excise if I could,
the part that objectifies these . . . , well, objects,
these figures that are, the problematic hair and fierce regard,
the unimpressive cock notwithstanding, timeless art.
Within the illusion of the timelessness of the universe,
the planets and the stars and more, art too
is illusion, and visual art, this statue of Perseus
and Medusa, perhaps the oldest kind. The young
Florentine man who modeled for Cellini
surely looked upon his representation with some rue,
but the model for Medusa—what did she think? Her body

sculpted and cast in bronze as a corpse and a monster.
But a beautiful dead monster she made. And it was
not the upright perfect left breast
that compelled me most, but the sole of her right foot,
a sole I could imagine (and may have) kissing,
attending to, praising, and more. It looked
like a sole I have kissed, attended to, praised, and more.
In this way Cellini, in his depiction of the aftermath
of Perseus's cunning and resourcefulness, gave me
just myself, far less cunning and not at all heroic,
juvenile in spite of and against my better judgment,
willing to unman a demigod
in the interests of myself, yes, but also of Medusa,
the only mortal one among the three sister Gorgons.
Now vastly impressive in all his other ways was Perseus,
but the myths of Medusa say her face was hideous
and turned men to stone. The face of Cellini's model
was surely no help to the artist in this regard.
He just needed her body, which was beautiful,
especially the sole of her right foot.
I might have mentioned that foot to Kim,
but only my admiration for it, no more.
And nothing about the rest of her body, nor about
Perseus and his small part in it all.

EVENING WEAR

Daylight slips into evening like a shirt,
blue of course, but one of those blues
the names of which are unfortunate,
even operatically overdone, like azure

or cerulean, so we'll just leave it blue.
Probably silk, though, or at least silken,
shiny, smooth, possibly diaphanous too.
(It might be sateen or maybe satin—

what's the difference?) Anyway,
day slips into its early evening shirt
and poses, or begins to drift away,
except now it's getting cool, so day starts

putting on a jacket (berry, indigo,
one of those), which will hide the contours
of its body just when we're about to know
if departing day is a woman or

a man or some beloved androgyne
worthy of the nightly advent of stars.
Late birds sing, the final whine
of insects diminishes, and somewhere

the full moon, feeling her enormous strength,
shoos departing day along with the dust,
and light, lithe in navy, slinks at length
toward the Pacific and Asia, as it must.

"WHY SHOULD THERE BE STARS?"

in memory of Wallace Roney
(May 25, 1960–March 31, 2020)

No one to talk to about it but a little bird, first
dusky flycatcher of the year, on the final day
of an eternal March. There's snow falling,
and the bird seems unmoved by that.

Perched on the lee side of the tree,
it's hunched and plumped,
but I've opened the window an inch,
so that it might listen with me to this mournful song.

It cocks its head when the trumpet comes in,
turns its body slightly, and its eyes look bright.
But its eyes always look bright and its song
isn't much. The field guide says its five notes
consist of *clip, whit, whee, wheep,* and *zee.*

But because it migrates mostly at night,
it knows why there should be stars.
And when the song ends, it bounces a bit
on the limb it's perched on and seems
to want to find a way to ask for more.

Today a great trumpeter died, at fifty-nine,
of the plague that blows across the earth,
and the little bird and I listen on.
Every time the song ends, I ask "Again?"
and the bird says zee, or whit, or wheep.

PRAISE HIM

How can the finch not know
the world he thinks he sees is just a window?
He knows but only in the last inch,
when a startling non-reflection glints
and the world-that-is shows
another into which a finch cannot go.

Soon there's a final finch flinch
and his gold degrades to chintz.
He's dead on the porch, losing his glow,
for the fancy vest of the goldfinch
fadeth in death it doth, since
impact so paled, it's hardly even yellow.

SONNET

Two ravens glide crosswise
down the wind, then slice
their way back and rise
into the brunt of the storm's ice
right before my human eyes,
each bird cawing twice—
but in code of course: there are spies
at large in their paradise

who hear something in these cries
half-contentious. To be precise,
one caw celebrates a carrion prize,
the other's an attempt to entice
that prize be shared, thus each flies,
haggling its raven asking price.

THE DOGS

How can the world which is
mostly stunned by you not be
stunned by you in every way?
The answer is, it is, but it is
as shy, the world, as the boy is
who could only show his love
by knocking you down on the playground.
Which explains how it is
you have been knocked down
so many times in your stunning life.
Tongue-tied boy world running
after you, inarticulate man world
mumbling its misplaced praises.
All praises are misplaced and needless.
Meanwhile, stunning, you go about
in more ways stunning than ever,
unaware how stunning your stunningness is.
Manifold the perplexities of this life.
Skin, for instance, the pirouettes
of intelligence, the lie detector an eye is.
Even the messed-up thumb knuckle
of your right hand—breathtaking.
The hamstring tendons back of the knees.
Eloquence, bravery. The tendency
to throw whomever you're with
between you and a snarling dog:
this too is known to be stunning.
Apotheosis of lips, syllables therefrom.
World says, There I am in you. World says,
You are the world that stuns the world,
the blue eyes that chasten its skies.

And the brown-eyed boys dying
for the lack of you, one dog,
another dog, one stunned after another,
believing they are the word for the world,
stunned that it is, like them, never true.

ACCOUNTING

Burgdorf Hot Springs, Perseids,
August 1982

Under a half-moon that night, the bull moose
might have thought that we, heeled together
on our inner tubes, were a pair of gigantic lily pads.

He came through the left-open gate
and clomped along the wooden walkway toward us,
his antlers casting shadows halfway across the pool.

When he stepped into the four-foot middle depths,
he stirred a wave that nearly capsized us
but paid us no mind at all, as we thrashed out

and scampered in the cold toward our clothes.
Instead he plunged his head again and again
into the hot water and flung from his horns

enormous starlit arcs of shimmering drops,
while we shivered in our towels and watched him
there, at the farthest, deepest end of the pool,

the water not quite reaching his dewlap. He blew
three blasts of breath from his flews and at last clambered out
at the meadow end, stepping over a yard-high fence

as though it were a city curb. He stood
in the star- and moonlight, steam rising from him
in a gauzy cape, before he walked

into the meadow itself, among the grazing elk
we'd been listening to for an hour,
so we dropped our towels and made our way

back to the inner tubes and stayed several hours more,
making love once, counting thirty-three meteors,
nine bull elk bugles, six cow barks, and a moose.

WHAT IT IS

Early morning sun just up, the mountains
a hundred miles south the very purple
the song insists they are, though the plains
are brittle with cold, dormant, stubbled,

unfruited but for the fallen grains geese
and pheasants all day long will probe for.
It's beautiful, the pink light from the east
over beautiful country, an Idaho blue norther

bearing down with a cargo of first snow
to complicate the eating habits of the birds.
Down the slope a ways, there's a doe
looking at the sky. There are words

for what she's thinking, I have no doubt,
words in the sudden wind she feels,
words she does not mourn being without,
words that watching never reveals,

but silent syllables made entirely of scent.
I would like to say what's on her mind
in her language and, in a line subsequent,
recite the blather and bluster of the wind

just as it pronounces itself now.
The doe's face in the face of it, my own
face bestreaked with tears somehow,
as the doe lies down behind a stone

and I go back inside and begin,
as sleet seals the northern window
and the wind says it is the wind,
while the snow insists it is only snow.

REGALIA

in memory of Bill Knott
(February 17, 1940–March 12, 2014)

Forlorn, the leather never-worn natty jacket
not quite crucified on the shoulder slope angel
angle of the hanger. This man jacket has no placket!
It's not like a shirt but a sort of mongrel

raiment, a fake mufti outfit unfit for arms,
neither chasuble nor alb, albeit a cowskin
reality, with a fealty to extravagant uniforms
and fruit salad inscrutable militaristic ribbons.

Attention! Let us to the will-of-the-good him give!
Let these unarmed arms ensleeve a thing or two,
let unto the yoke and armscye arrive
the fishspear arrowhand fist, I implore you,

so that he, brave jacket, may go forth, emblem
of what he has been to us, as vestments were to him.

ACKUMPUCKY

November 1, 2016

A noxious-scented glue
used to affix fabric or leather
to smooth fiberboard or metal, color
of radioactive tea. Or sap

from the cherry tree, or some sort
of industrial spreadable-cheese product
he'd apply to a slice of white bread
with the same care and coverage

he used with the glue.
Brylcreem too, to shellac his hair
into its single rightward wave.
That was what he called them all.

Any sticky, tacky, mucilaginous, agglutinative,
or tenacious substance, all his life long,
he referred to as ackumpucky.
"Hand me that ackumpucky," he'd say.

Over the years I had thought it one
of his personal locutions—like *marble forest*
for the cemetery, or *kertwocky,* an onomatopoeic
coinage far superior to *pow* or *wham* or *boom.*

Here's yet another annoying thing about the internet,
all things searchable and seemingly thereon—
not even the *OED* includes this word! But there it is,
name of a corporation registered in San Antonio, Texas,

which, according to that state's attorney general,
is "not in good standing," whatever on earth
that might mean in Texas. This ridiculous word
I thought he had invented came to me

this morning, after I'd sat drinking coffee
on the porch, watching a black-headed grosbeak
rifle the feeder for thistle seed, when I rose,
or attempted to, from the chair, only to find

I'd been sitting on a pancake of pitch
fallen from a big yellow pine onto the seat.
And the chair rose with me, dangled
from my backside a second, then clattered

back to the wood it had sat on, leaving long,
opaque, and gelatinous filaments between us.
Then I said "ackumpucky" and thought of him,
my father, dead exactly twenty-seven months that day.

COWRAN

Kooskooskia Meadows, Selway-Bitterroot Wilderness

From beneath a leaf under the full moon
a twitched tail electrified the owl.
Or so, seated on a log, I imagined.
I had only the owl's tenoroon call

to place it by, and the meadow
before me aquake with timorousness
and teeming, when the horned owl glided
silent as a star over still grasses

and fell upon its prey, God's hooks, God's hooks.
Jesus, had He been there, might have sipped
and sighed and swallowed with me from my flask,
having witnessed the great horned owl's wing tips

ignited by the white light of a moon
men have walked on, though He might have asked why.
Even without Jesus, I was not alone.
With me, a mouse, a moon, an owl, the sky.

How could predation be so spectacular?
What was the point of walking on the moon?
Why camp way out here, or walk on water?
Three minutes later the owl called again.

June meadow grasses trembled silver.
God warned, do not blink, twitch, or even breathe.
In such silence did creation quiver
under the moon, under each dewy shimmering leaf.

THREE OCTAVES

1. YOU ARE GETTING SLEEPY

Outside the window, up the tree a ways, the hawk
holds the carcass of a rabbit down
against a branch and tears its flesh and beaks
the viscera in, and the rabbit's mournful frown

changes not at all as its guts and lungs and heart
are devoured, but when I stand the better to see,
the hawk sees me and stops, as some viscous part
of bloody rabbit dangles and, swinging, hypnotizes me.

2. WAITING FOR THE SNOW TO KILL THE SLUGS, IN THE INTERESTS OF THE LAST STRAWBERRIES

An ordinary early fall inclemency, this
quarter inch of wet, heavy snow,
but among the chipmunks' mad circuits
a singular grooved track also shows.

And here it is in its long curved course—
a slug nearing the lowest leaf.
How are you not yet dead, jelly bean horse,
oleaginous one, cold unsalted thief?

3. GUSTY

On the way to the wedding the crowd
of groomsmen is stripped of their lichen boutonnieres
by a wind not quite a gale but stout,
all the chartreuse blossoms blown here and there.

Then come down on the deck a perfect loop
of mint-green tree moss called old-man's beard,
which blows away just as I stoop
to get it, like the fragrant rustic garter of the bride.

FALLING OFF HE DEVIL

Seven Devils Wilderness, July 1980

Such a swift but elongated four or five seconds,
skidding on my back down the snowfield,
hoping to catch myself with a plant
of my boots on a slant of stone
at the end of the snow.

But no, momentum launched me
into the air and spun me over
a full three hundred sixty degrees,
so that I landed heels and back-flat first
in cold muck and pea gravel accumulated

by snowmelt. A perfect trajectory, it turned out,
since two feet right or left of where I landed
were jagged and pulverizing pinions
and cogs, granite shards and boulders
that would have bashed my bones to pulp.

A miracle, forty years ago.
Although now and then ever since
a speck of shiny gravel oozes
up from my backflesh like an ordinary pimple
but with a core of stone

my wife squeezes free for me.
I place it with the others
in a tiny brass snuffbox

that once belonged to my grandmother,
who in all the born days of her life

never set eyes on a mountain,
nor cared to.

WATCHING A LANDSLIDE

Sawtooth Wilderness, 2006

Irregular at first, a few rocks dislodge
and staccato down the slope of scree
across the lake, until the whole friable face
sags in a squashed rhombus,

then blasts and buries the shoreline baluster boulders
all the way to their boulder shoulders, baby—

after which a trapezoidal cloud of dust rises
and drifts limp as a severed blossom

until silence returns, and a breeze,
followed by the chop of newly hewn waves,
which roll across the surface to lap exuberant
and washed of all dust at our feet.

HIM DADDY

He understood she understood
something about him, a boy
on the last ledge of boyhood—
that the plummet he could not perceive rushing
out from under him would be rushing out
from under him soon. She understood
he understood nothing but might do anything
he was asked and so asked of him nothing.
Shirtless on the shady porch, little dark coronas
of chest hair come on round his nipples, he drank
an RC Cola, she an ice tea. His shut-down mower
ticked in the sun as he swirled the icy bottom
of the bottle around his chest and belly
and addressed her as Mrs. D. and she did
not correct him but regarded him
with mysterious frankness,
a sandal dangled from her red-painted toes.
This made him remember he'd been supposed to
ask if she wanted more tomatoes
but there was his mother anyway,
crossing the street with a bowlful,
smiling and saying hi and reminding him
he'd got to do the Reimlers' lawn too
and Daddy would be home in a couple of hours,
although he hadn't called him Daddy in years.

SHE SAID

on the fifty-eighth anniversary

Friday, English class, seventh grade.
        Nearly everyone alive that day remembers
where they were and will until they die.
        When the intercom announcement came,
we were diagramming sentences, one of the few
        things I understood and was good at in school.

We would not know for many years,
        not until the Secret Service man who
covered her body with his own reported
        that the president's wife spoke to her murdered husband
in the back seat of a convertible limousine.
        She said, Oh, Jack, what have they done?

I wonder if sentence diagramming was over
        for the day at that point, which would have
disappointed me, since I was good at it
        and doing it made me feel smart
and understand certain things—
        the machine, the organism, the symbols of the words
arranged just so, doing what they did. Everyone
        in that convertible limousine that day
is dead now, except for the Secret Service man.
        He has remembered what she said all his life since.

We stayed in school
        until the final bell, then walked or rode
a school bus home. I don't remember. But everyone
        alive then remembers when the man

they said had fired the shots was shot himself,

       two days later, at the Dallas police station. We watched it

over and over and over on TV.

       The day after that I saw my father cry

for the only time in my life. He lay on the sofa,

       watching a state funeral in black-and-white

between his stockinged feet. When the band played

       the Navy Hymn, he began to cry.

Outside all the leaves had fallen from the trees.

       There were no birds.

The TV announcers explained the symbolism

       of Black Jack, the riderless horse,

and of the six gray horses pulling the caisson

       that held the casket. In the post-shooting chaos,

her pink pillbox hat was lost.

Someone has that hat, we don't know who.

       A strawberry pink, wool bouclé, double-breasted

Chanel suit, she wore it the rest of the day

       as it stiffened with her husband's blood.

She said she regretted she'd washed the blood

       from her face before the swearing in of LBJ.

She said she wanted them

       to see what they had done to Jack.

They had done what

       they had done and my father cried

and I went outside and walked around

       and did not climb any trees,

although they offered themselves to me.

       All I did was walk. There were no birds

anywhere. A cold, late November day.

       I wasn't wearing a coat

but didn't want to go inside,
        until I was sure my father was finished.
It was thought when she climbed
        in her smart suit out onto the trunk lid
of the Lincoln, that she meant to help
        the Secret Service man into the car.
That may have been when she lost her hat.

In fact, she climbed out
        to retrieve a chunk of her husband's skull.
Sixteen years after she died,
        Agent Clint Hill, who is still alive,
gave the interview in which he repeated
        what she said—Oh, Jack, what have they done?
He was shielding her body.
        Her hat was gone, her lips
just touching her dead husband's ear.
        A sentence. A rhetorical question.
In the noise and clamor, no one else heard.

I'm not sure I knew there was such a thing
        as a rhetorical question at twelve,
but I could have diagrammed hers.
        The subject is *they*.
It would have been placed at the
        left end of a horizontal line and separated
from the verb, *have done*,
        by a perpendicular line. On the right, the object,
separated by yet another perpendicular line: *what*.
        In this way the sentence,
interrogatory, is turned to a declarative statement:
        They have done what.
They, third person plural pronoun,
        refers to a group not specifically identified.

What, a relative pronoun, also refers
        to something unstated,
unless it is blood and bone, her husband's
        exploded head in her lap,
nothing more, and no one else.

CHORUS

She wasn't there when I began to play,
and it's a song I haven't played since page eight,
so it requires a little extra concentration from me,

which is why she seems so suddenly just to be there—
appearing in the empty space before
the porch of the shack and looking up

and most of all listening. For deer always listen.
They can hear you lick your lips
fifty yards away, it is said, and I'm reaching

the second time through the chorus now,
which consists mostly of the repeated title,
and "yeah-yeah-yeah." The thing is, as usual

I've slowed the song way down, and I'm fingerpicking,
not pounding with a pick, and with its three
minor chords, it sounds almost like a ballad,

or slow and sad, at least. Even the yeah-yeah-yeahs,
I admit, I try to work a little extra from.
So, yeah, it occurs to me that, indeed, I am performing

for a deer. And I want her not only to appreciate
the miraculous fact of human music but also of me.
Performing for her, hell. I'm playing

and singing *to* her, all the while aware—
despite her beauty, her impossibly big brown eyes,
her listening—that it would never work out between us.

It's a mild day in late autumn. She's probably pregnant,
I'm as old as half the trees around us.
But the look on her face is so intense, so pure

in its regard, that it feels like everything else in the world
has gone to that place everything else in the world goes to
when you are looked at that way, especially

if you're singing, and the worst thing
that could happen at such a time is for the song to end.
So I keep on singing "She loves you, yeah-yeah-yeah."

ACKNOWLEDGMENTS

The author offers his grateful acknowledgment to the editors of the following periodicals in which these poems first appeared, now and then in somewhat different form or under different titles:

Alaska Quarterly Review: "Bison"; "Horse Heaven"

The American Journal of Poetry: "An Everywhere at Once"; "Be Glad"; "Old Pan"; "Praise Him"; "Regalia"; "What It Means" (as "Wing"); "Why the Night Bird Sings"

Ascent: "After a Long Dry Spell"; "Done"; "Rodeo"

Bennington Review: "The Dogs"

Bracken: "Black and White"

Conduit: "What It Is" (as "Mend Thine Ev'ry Flaw")

Copper Nickel: "Moss Loves Bone to Death"

decomp: "Prothalamion"

EcoTheo Review: "Cowran"

Fugue: "Barn"

The Georgia Review: "Lovely"; "Machinery"; "What It's Good For" (as "16 Down")

The Harvard Advocate: "Synovial"

The London Magazine: "To the Man"

Mānoa: "The Flower of All Water"; "Prey"

Mantis: "Bone Pile"

Mudlark: "The Consciousness of Everything"

Northwest Review: "Hummingbird on the Wire"

Poetry: "Figure"; "Might Have Been July, Might Have Been December"

Rattle: "'Why Should There Be Stars?'"

River Styx: "Visitant"

Sierra (the Magazine of the Sierra Club): "Watching a Landslide"

Solstice: "Perseus with the Head of Medusa"

Terrain.org: "Accounting"; "Come Home"; "Dawn"; "Upper Walton Lake"; "I Want to Praise Her Parts"

Under a Warm Green Linden: "How Enormous"

Vox Populi: "Narrating Night to the New Puppy Gladys"; "She Said" (as "What She Said")

Waxwing: "Chorus"

"AK-47 Candelabrum" first appeared in *Bullets into Bells: Poets and Citizens Respond to Gun Violence*, Brian Clements, Alexandra Teague, and Dean Rader, editors (Boston: Beacon Press, 2017).

"Machinery" was reprinted in *The Best American Poetry 2020*, selected by Paisley Rekdal; David Lehman, series editor (New York: Scribner, 2020).

Thanks especially to Kim Barnes, Dan Gerber, Ron McFarland, and Georgia Tiffany, who read many of these poems in early drafts and offered invaluable advice.

Visit **robertwrigley.com**.

ROBERT WRIGLEY has won numerous awards for his work, including the Kingsley Tufts Poetry Award, the San Francisco Poetry Center Book Award, and a Pacific Northwest Book Award. He lives in the woods of Idaho, with his wife, the writer Kim Barnes. *The True Account of Myself as a Bird* is his twelfth collection of poems. He is also the author of a collection of personal essays, mostly about poetry, called *Nemerov's Door.*

GAROUS ABDOLMALEKIAN
Lean Against This Late Hour

PAIGE ACKERSON-KIELY
Dolefully, A Rampart Stands

JOHN ASHBERY
Selected Poems
Self-Portrait in a Convex Mirror

PAUL BEATTY
Joker, Joker, Deuce

JOSHUA BENNETT
Owed
The Sobbing School

TED BERRIGAN
The Sonnets

LAUREN BERRY
The Lifting Dress

JOE BONOMO
Installations

PHILIP BOOTH
Lifelines: Selected Poems 1950–1999
Selves

JIM CARROLL
Fear of Dreaming: The Selected Poems
Living at the Movies
Void of Course

RIO CORTEZ
Golden Ax

ALISON HAWTHORNE DEMING
Genius Loci
Rope
Stairway to Heaven

CARL DENNIS
Another Reason
Callings
Earthborn
New and Selected Poems 1974–2004
Night School
Practical Gods
Ranking the Wishes
Unknown Friends

DIANE DI PRIMA
Loba

STUART DISCHELL
Backwards Days
Dig Safe

STEPHEN DOBYNS
Velocities: New and Selected Poems 1966–1992

EDWARD DORN
Way More West

HEID E. ERDRICH
Little Big Bully

ROGER FANNING
The Middle Ages

ADAM FOULDS
The Broken Word: An Epic Poem of the British Empire in Kenya, and the Mau Mau Uprising Against It

CARRIE FOUNTAIN
Burn Lake
Instant Winner
The Life

AMY GERSTLER
Dearest Creature
Ghost Girl
Index of Women
Medicine
Nerve Storm
Scattered at Sea

EUGENE GLORIA
Drivers at the Short-Time Motel
Hoodlum Birds
My Favorite Warlord
Sightseer in This Killing City

DEBORA GREGER
In Darwin's Room

ZEINA HASHEM BECK
O

TERRANCE HAYES
American Sonnets for My Past and Future Assassin
Hip Logic
How to Be Drawn
Lighthead
Wind in a Box

NATHAN HOKS
The Narrow Circle

ROBERT HUNTER
Sentinel and Other Poems

MARY KARR
Viper Rum

WILLIAM KECKLER
Sanskrit of the Body

JACK KEROUAC
Book of Blues
Book of Haikus
Book of Sketches

JOANNA KLINK
Circadian
Excerpts from a Secret Prophecy
The Nightfields
Raptus

JOANNE KYGER
As Ever: Selected Poems

PENGUIN POETS

ANN LAUTERBACH
Hum
If in Time:
  Selected Poems
  1975–2000
On a Stair
Or to Begin Again
Spell
Under the Sign

CORINNE LEE
Plenty
Pyx

PHILLIS LEVIN
May Day
Mercury
Mr. Memory
  & Other Poems

PATRICIA LOCKWOOD
Motherland Fatherland
  Homelandsexuals

WILLIAM LOGAN
Rift of Light

J. MICHAEL MARTINEZ
Museum of the Americas

ADRIAN MATEJKA
The Big Smoke
Map to the Stars
Mixology
Somebody Else Sold
  the World

MICHAEL McCLURE
Huge Dreams: San Francisco
  and Beat Poems

ROSE McLARNEY
Forage
Its Day Being Gone

DAVID MELTZER
David's Copy:
  The Selected Poems
  of David Meltzer

TERESA K. MILLER
Borderline Fortune

ROBERT MORGAN
Dark Energy
Terroir

CAROL MUSKE-DUKES
Blue Rose
An Octave Above Thunder:
  New and Selected Poems
Red Trousseau
Twin Cities

ALICE NOTLEY
Certain Magical Acts
Culture of One
The Descent of Alette
Disobedience
For the Ride
In the Pines
Mysteries of Small Houses

WILLIE PERDOMO
The Crazy Bunch
The Essential Hits
  of Shorty Bon Bon

DANIEL POPPICK
Fear of Description

LIA PURPURA
It Shouldn't Have Been
  Beautiful

LAWRENCE RAAB
The History of Forgetting

BARBARA RAS
The Last Skin
One Hidden Stuff

MICHAEL ROBBINS
Alien vs. Predator
The Second Sex
Walkman

PATTIANN ROGERS
Generations
Holy Heathen Rhapsody
Quickening Fields
Wayfare

SAM SAX
Madness

ROBYN SCHIFF
A Woman of Property

WILLIAM STOBB
Absentia
Nervous Systems

TRYFON TOLIDES
An Almost Pure Empty
  Walking

VINCENT TORO
Tertulia

PAUL TRAN
All the Flowers Kneeling

SARAH VAP
Viability

ANNE WALDMAN
Gossamurmur
Kill or Cure
Manatee/Humanity
Trickster Feminism

JAMES WELCH
Riding the Earthboy 40

PHILIP WHALEN
Overtime: Selected Poems

PHILLIP B. WILLIAMS
Mutiny

ROBERT WRIGLEY
Anatomy of Melancholy
  and Other Poems
Beautiful Country
Box
Earthly Meditations:
  New and Selected Poems
Lives of the Animals
Reign of Snakes
The True Account of Myself
  as a Bird

MARK YAKICH
The Importance of Peeling
  Potatoes in Ukraine
Spiritual Exercises
Unrelated Individuals
  Forming a Group Waiting
  to Cross